PECULIAR PETS

Creative Verse

Edited By Roseanna Caswell

First published in Great Britain in 2021 by:

Young Writers
Remus House
Coltsfoot Drive
Peterborough
PE2 9BF
Telephone: 01733 890066
Website: www.youngwriters.co.uk

All Rights Reserved
Book Design by Ashley Janson
© Copyright Contributors 2020
Softback ISBN 978-1-80015-123-9

Printed and bound in the UK by BookPrintingUK
Website: www.bookprintinguk.com
YB0453F

FOREWORD

Welcome Reader!

Are you ready to discover weird and wonderful creatures that you'd never even dreamed of?

For Young Writers' latest competition we asked primary school pupils to create a Peculiar Pet of their own invention, and then write a poem about it! They rose to the challenge magnificently and the result is this fantastic collection full of creepy critters and amazing animals!

Here at Young Writers our aim is to encourage creativity in children and to inspire a love of the written word, so it's great to get such an amazing response, with some absolutely fantastic poems. Not only have these young authors created imaginative and inventive animals, they've also crafted wonderful poems to showcase their creations and their writing ability. These poems are brimming with inspiration. The slimiest slitherers, the creepiest crawlers and furriest friends are all brought to life in these pages – you can decide for yourself which ones you'd like as a pet!

I'd like to congratulate all the young authors in this anthology, I hope this inspires them to continue with their creative writing.

✶ CONTENTS ✶

All Saints CE Primary School, Marple

Maddie Ormerod (7)	1
Felix Dine (7)	2
Eden H-S (7)	3
Amy Jervis (7)	4
Polly Dine (7)	5
Emily Cater (7)	6
Harmony Dunkerley (7)	7
Mason Andrasson (7)	8
Rio Sohrvardi (8)	9
Ella Drake (7)	10
Emilia Clyne (7)	11
Regan Doherty (8)	12
Max Ensinger (8)	13
Robin Clark (8)	14
Archie Hegg (7)	15
Tyler O'Hara (8)	16
Benji Hopkin-Green (7)	17

Appleton Wiske CP School, Appleton Wiske

Dougal Gaudie (10)	18
Sophia Bateson (8)	19
Daisy Wilson (7)	20
Rose Rountree (8)	21
Kayden Michael Andrew Hodgson (11)	22
Haiden Patel (9)	23
Daniel Thomas James Green (11)	24
Avery Brook (9)	25
John Richard Cassidy (8)	26
Sophie Connolly (10)	27

Joshua Ring (8)	28
Bethany Ring (10)	29
Edward Stainthorpe (7)	30
Alice King (8)	31
Katie Hutchinson (10)	32
Sophie Elizabeth Green (9)	33
Eva Mae Pearce (7)	34
Robert Roe (8)	35
Rosie Wilson (9)	36
Violet Rose Ellison (8)	37
Bobby Ross (8)	38
Riley William Michael Jackson (10)	39
Lily Easby (7)	40
Hattie Pattison (9)	41
Isabelle King (8)	42
Jake Graham (8)	43
Poppy Race (9)	44
Charlie Stainthorpe (10)	45
Jack Gibson (7)	46
Ellie McGuigan (8)	47
Anouska Brook (7)	48

Bantock Primary School, Penn Fields

Anum Bashir (9)	49
Thalia Harris (8)	50
Riley-James Proctor-Williams (8)	51
Joshua-James Bennett (8)	52
Jessica Kaur (9)	53
Catalina Bouros (9)	54

Bedlington Station Primary School, Bedlington

Kasey Humble (11)	55
Kirah Obrien (10)	56
Millie Barker (10)	57
Nathan Leif Uddgren-Barham (10)	58
Liam Stanton (10)	59
Evie Moat (10)	60
Ethan Loy (10)	61
Kolby Carrick (11)	62
Harry Mason (10)	63
Levi Graham (10)	64
Josh Bell (10)	65
Aiden Falloon (10)	66
Charlie Ullock (10)	67
Dean Foster (10)	68
Phoebe Macneish (10)	69
Jack Simpson (10)	70
Hallie Taylor (10)	71

Cale Green Primary School, Shaw Heath

Shanzeh Khan (7)	72
Tilly Lee (7)	73

Chase House School, Brownhills

A M (8)	74
Beau Reading (8)	75

Hillington Primary School, Hillington

Eve Millar (11)	76
Abigail Sarah McMahon (10)	77
Dylan Burns (12)	78
Lucy McLean (11)	79
Rhiannon McFadden (10)	80
Aston Daly (10)	81
Isha Zaheer (10)	82
Maisie McLaughlin (10)	83
Aaliyah Sinclair (11)	84
Alexa Ingram (11)	85
Kayla Mullin (10)	86
Rebecca Burns (9)	87
Myley McFlynn (11)	88
Liam Elliot (9)	89
Aidan Lindsay (10)	90
Ellie Rae Stewart (11)	91
Jack Sherriff (10)	92
Stephen Smith (10)	93
Lewis Brown (11)	94
Hollie Kinnear (11)	95
Mirren McGregor (10)	96
Brooke Lipsett (11)	97
Brooke Lang (10)	98
Ava Brown (10)	99

Holme CE Primary Academy, Holme

Owen Vinton (9)	100
Jessica Hume (9)	102
Loretta Davis (9)	103
Ben Leschallas (10)	104
Bella Marshall (9)	105
Noah Weston (10)	106
Ben Oliver Burks (10)	107
Zion Mugabo (10)	108
Harry Chapman (10)	109
Dylan Stevenson (9)	110
Noah Dyball (10)	111
Keeley Welch (10)	112
Vito Max Wolsing (10)	113
Eli Colam (10)	114
Ayden Pattison (10)	115
Elie Connell (10)	116

Johnson Fold Community Primary School, Bolton

Riley Stobbs (9)	117
Harrison Bond (9)	118
Charlie Greenhalgh (9)	119
Athena Mckenzie (9)	120
Katie Newton (10)	121

Lily Pennington (9)	122
Chloe Louise Gregson (9)	123
Faye Bourke, Rach & Tomasz Sadzik (9)	124
Kacie Smith (10)	125

Mill Of Mains Primary School, Dundee

Amy Robbins (10)	126
Lacey Stewart (10)	127
Qais Naseer (11)	128
Lacey Murphy (9)	129
Aimie Milne (10)	130
Alix Sutherland (10)	131
Madison Adams (9)	132
Callum Carson (9)	133
Mylah Dodds-Jackson (10)	134
Ava Egan (10)	135
Autumn Iannetta (10)	136
Brèagha Stewart (9)	137
Noah Snee (10)	138
Rosco McBride (10)	139
Mylie Watt (10)	140
Ollie Sime (9)	141
Lenny Christie (10)	142
Elly-May Mann (10)	143
Logan Smith (10)	144
Harry Scott (10)	145
Jude Ferrie (10)	146

St Mary's RC Primary School, Swinton

Rafael Corona (9)	147
Jack Burton (10)	148
Olivia Seddon (10)	150
Oscar Tomlinson (9)	152
Ellana Fahy (9)	153
Maisie-Rae Foster (9)	154
Annie McKiernan (10)	155
Nathan Rolfe (10)	156
Orla Bramble (9)	157
George Kinman (9)	158

Jake Bird (9)	159
Alfie Fanning (9)	160
Poppy Fletcher (10)	161
Alex Kavanagh (9)	162
Sophie Fountain (9)	163
Rebekah Coates (9)	164
Isabella Gudice (9)	165
Fabiana Race (9)	166
Finn Mailey (9)	167
Kalan Williams (9)	168
Harvey-Jay Mungins (10)	169
Nicholas Bosak (9)	170
Dawid Rachwal (10)	171
Lucy Dyer (9)	172

St Michael With St Thomas Primary School, Widnes

Amelia Williams (10)	173
Ellis Welding (10)	174
Summer Cowen (10)	175
Hayden Vallender (10)	176
Evie Halkett (10)	177
India Mullarkey (10)	178
Max Jones (10)	179
Sean Mcloughlin (11)	180
Phoebe Price (11)	181
Elise Highfield (10)	182
Holly Hart (10)	183

THE POEMS

The Moon Doggy

I adopted a dog.
She was cute and furry.
At full moon, she flies away with me and goes back in the morning at 6am.
At full sunset, she howls like a wolf.
We wait until night, when Mum is in bed,
Then I jump on her back and fly to space.
One day, she taught me how to fly.
Then we flew together every night.
It was like a miracle.
No one knew what sort of dog she was.
Everyone thought she was a rare one that no one knew.
She was a mysterious, rare, flying dog!
She did a mysterious howl and it was like she was talking to her dog family.

Maddie Ormerod (7)
All Saints CE Primary School, Marple

Rockstar Cat

R ockstar Cat is as cool as a cucumber
O range chocolate is Rockstar Cat's favourite food
C ats love Rockstar Cat
K indhearted Rockstar Cat has thousands of fans
S tar is how cats describe him
T he style of Rockstar Cat amazes cats
A fter his show, cats always want more
R oyal cats invite him to their birthdays

C antering around the stage, Rockstar Cat sings
A mazing cats praise him
T he crowd goes wild.

Felix Dine (7)
All Saints CE Primary School, Marple

Flying Timy Rap

F lying Timy is a marvellous pet
L ying in the sun waiting for his wings to stretch
Y ay, my marvellous pet is the best
I love him, he is the best, no one will beat him
N aughty and makes a pretty good guard dog
G ood and the best

T imy is the best
I love him with all my heart
M y marvellous pet
Y ay!

P.S. A marvellous dog needs a marvellous cat,
Her name is Mrs Whiskers and that is that!

Eden H-S (7)
All Saints CE Primary School, Marple

Wow! What A Pet!

Wow! What a pet, it is really cool
She can fly above high trees and never gets fleas

She sometimes is a mess but really she's a pest
So come and join us and fly above the high sky

Her name is Sparkle
She really does spark when you touch her horn
She really does burn
She has loads of friends
They're really nice
She sparks, burns and twirls

So come and join us and fly above the high sky.

Amy Jervis (7)
All Saints CE Primary School, Marple

My Little Fox

My little fox is the cutest of all
My little fox can lead the way in the dark
I love my little fox
I can ride on my little fox over the sea
My little fox is the best
My little fox is as soft as a pillow
I like my little fox
My little fox can warm up my feet when they're cold
My little fox is the best.

Polly Dine (7)
All Saints CE Primary School, Marple

The Unicorn That Could Talk

My pet is a unicorn
It is peculiar because it can talk
Every night, I go in the garden and see her
She takes me up on her back
She likes to see me after I come back from school
She's so pretty and she has a yellow horn
It sparkles in the night
It wakes me up and that's when it's time to play.

Emily Cater (7)
All Saints CE Primary School, Marple

Moo, The Grumpy Cat

One day I got a cat
She was named Snowball
We had her for a year
Then we got a new cat named Waffle
They had babies
We had ten kittens and guess what?
We kept one
We named her Moo Dunkley
Because she looked like a cow
She had superpowers
She wore her little suit every day.

Harmony Dunkerley (7)
All Saints CE Primary School, Marple

The Big Griffin

B ig griffin is as big as the moon
I t comes out at night
G reat big claws

G iggles when you tickle his tummy
R eally loves the night
I t is friendly
F antastic
F riend
I t is an amazing pet
N ight is its home.

Mason Andrasson (7)
All Saints CE Primary School, Marple

Griffin

G riffin always, when I am sad, he makes me happy
R azor-sharp beak, I nickname him
I love Griffin with all my heart
F antastic wings of Griffin are very giant
F antasy Griffin is mythical
I am proud of Griffin
N aughty Griffin.

Rio Sohrvardi (8)
All Saints CE Primary School, Marple

Flying Pig

This is my peculiar pet, Honey
She is a flying pig
She is very cute, like a unicorn
She does not have sharp teeth
She does not get angry with you
She does not bite
She is my dream come true
She can dance
She only comes out at night
I love her.

Ella Drake (7)
All Saints CE Primary School, Marple

The Flying Elephant

He flies high, passing by in the night sky
I can see him in the sky
Twirling and whirling and swirling
What a fantastic little flying elephant
He flies by, he sneezes
The feather makes him sneeze
And then he flies
It was a very long way to go.

Emilia Clyne (7)
All Saints CE Primary School, Marple

Hi

Hi doesn't like to play nice
He shoots lasers out of his eyes
He is lazy and eats daisies
He only flies at night and goes to the moon
He has parties with his family
When he goes back to Earth
He gets a phone and plays on it.

Regan Doherty (8)
All Saints CE Primary School, Marple

Mr Raccoon

My raccoon is called Joe
He is no normal raccoon
You see, my raccoon loves discos
I will tell you about how he became who he is now
Joe went to a disco and played the mixing decks
That's how he got to who he is now.

Max Ensinger (8)
All Saints CE Primary School, Marple

My Hairy Frog

You have to be crazy to have a frog, like me
He's hairy, he has rocket boosters
He's crazy, but also my best friend
We go to space and different countries
I like going to Italy because they have really good food.

Robin Clark (8)
All Saints CE Primary School, Marple

The Flipanika

Once there was a fairy
It was very energetic and very humongous
It looked very weird
It spoke French
Its name was Flipanika
When it is friends with you, it protects you.

Archie Hegg (7)
All Saints CE Primary School, Marple

The Chicken

The chicken only comes out at night
The chicken makes a noise
It has a chick
The chick is cute
The chickens are quiet in the day
But at night they go out to play.

Tyler O'Hara (8)
All Saints CE Primary School, Marple

The Cat Who Fell Off The Cliff

The cat fell off the cliff
He was falling and falling
Until he was stuck
Then he was saved
And everyone cheered
Then he teleported back home.

Benji Hopkin-Green (7)
All Saints CE Primary School, Marple

Super Mayan Dog

S cared sloths run away
U nusual animals bolt out of the rainforest
P eter, the Mayan warrior, arrived riding on a giant dog
E veryone ran as the fire-breathing animal came
"R un!" screamed a Mayan, as a foot like a temple flattened him like a newspaper hitting a fly

"M ayan Dog is my name!" howled the great beast
A Mayan chief fainted when he saw the obsidian teeth
"Y oma Man!" a rapper called, as he was stood on
A scary song shook the skin as Peter fried the warrior king
N ow this made the warriors angry, they caught Peter's hanky panky

"D ig, dig, dig, I am no pig," yelled the big dog
"O ooohaaa!"
"G rr!" went the dog.

Dougal Gaudie (10)
Appleton Wiske CP School, Appleton Wiske

Evil Elephant

E very day he puts his jetpack on... *whoosh!*
V ery mischievous and has superpowers
I t loves to start mischief and crime
L ikes to attack and his claws are as sharp as a cactus

E vil Elephant is colossal and really, really grumpy
L ittle does anyone know he is moody
E vil Elephant is really good at doing amazing tricks
P ancakes for breakfast, that's what he likes for energy
H e is as big as a massive, snowy mountain
A fter superhero pets go to get him... he turns into a giant!
N ot nice to animals and super evil
T errifying and everyone stays away from him.

Sophia Bateson (8)
Appleton Wiske CP School, Appleton Wiske

Marvellous Mircat

M arvellous Mircat isn't so marvellous
A nnoying Mircat is so boring
R osie his girlfriend is beautiful
V ery strong Mircat can punch you to the ground
E mily, their little girl planted the garden
L ovely flowers
L ike water
O n the bus their family gets
"U se your bus pass," Rosie said
S mell the jungle with your nose

M ircat has not got a big brain
I don't like him, he smells
R osie is back
C ome and see
A t home he is rich
T en today, Emily is.

Daisy Wilson (7)
Appleton Wiske CP School, Appleton Wiske

Dancing Giraffe

D ancing giraffes are very rare
A nd very good at dancing
N ot so good at singing because they are a bit squeaky
C lever at dancing and tricks
I ncredible dancing tricks like a magician
N ice and kind to other animals
G looming and shimmering, the golden boots he wore

G limmering as the sun shines on his boots
I like dancing and prancing as the day goes on
R ound and round he dances
A dancing giraffe I am
F antastic at dancing
F antastic at prancing
E xcellent at dancing he is.

Rose Rountree (8)
Appleton Wiske CP School, Appleton Wiske

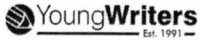

The Stupid Snake

Have you ever seen a stupid snake?
I've seen one on the way to school
It was waving its head like a wand
Before whacking a pole with a rake

As it went on, it stopped
Oh, he is as black as the void
He is a goldfish not being able to think
It started raining cats and dogs and then he flopped

He turned and started licking a hen
Then trying to eat a bench and a pole
The snake stopped and went to the water
Then he was never seen again.

Kayden Michael Andrew Hodgson (11)
Appleton Wiske CP School, Appleton Wiske

The Egyptian Mummy Chick Cool Dude

C ool Chicki likes lightning
O h, he is a bit frightening
O ww! He stood on me like a horse
L ow music, that's not cool, *beat, beat!*

C ool Chicki is a cheater
H e is the coolest chick around town, *chic, chic!*
I t never ever gives a frown
C ool Chicki is an Egyptian mummy
K o! Sometimes that happens to his tummy
I wonder what his actual name is?

Haiden Patel (9)
Appleton Wiske CP School, Appleton Wiske

The Naughty Dog

T he naughty dog
H e has never got stuck in a log
E arrings pink

N ever stinks
A s good at driving as a cop
U ltra-fast speed, saying "I won't stop!"
G uns and loot
H e has black as coal boots
T he wind howled at him
Y ellow and blue pencils he threw in the bin

D etermined but strong
O ranges make him pong
G reat at being naughty.

Daniel Thomas James Green (11)
Appleton Wiske CP School, Appleton Wiske

Unidragon

U nique Unidragon is as tiny as an ant
N ose breathing bubbles like a bubble blaster
I ncredible flying like a parrot swooshing through the trees
D angerous like a dinosaur eating leaves
R ed and as bright as the sun at sunset
A dorable like a kitten's cute eyes
G rumpy like an old man watching TV
O n the night-time he hunts for food for his family
N othing can stop him from flying in the air.

Avery Brook (9)
Appleton Wiske CP School, Appleton Wiske

Super Turtle

My turtle and I fly through the sky,
Turtle is as big as a mammoth,
We see people taking the jewellery,
Whoosh! We chased them,
We ran as quick as a flash,
We tried to cut them off,
We tried to overtake them,
We were out of luck,
Then as quick as a flash,
We had an idea,
We cut them off and waited,
Then we peeked around the corner,
Then we stopped them,
We grabbed them,
Received the jewellery and put it back.

John Richard Cassidy (8)
Appleton Wiske CP School, Appleton Wiske

Striperster

My peculiar pet
Was caught in a radioactive net
Her heart is gold
And she's soft to hold
Striperster is as cute as a teddy bear
With very scruffy hair
She is so cute
And she plays the flute
During the night
When the stars are bright
She flies into the sky
Up, up high
During the day Striperster is the size of a football
Which is so small
Later, Striperster is the size of a tree
When she goes off to ski.

Sophie Connolly (10)
Appleton Wiske CP School, Appleton Wiske

George The Galactic Gecko

George the galactic gecko,
Does like drinking prosecco.
He shot down from space,
And said it was a nice place.
He does like making an echo.
His feet go off like a full charged rocket,
Sometimes I think he needs a socket.
He wears a helmet,
But does not have a pelmet.
His favourite colour is yellow.
He has a moustache,
And boy, he can dash.
Bing, bing,
Is how they sing.
George is a magician.

Joshua Ring (8)
Appleton Wiske CP School, Appleton Wiske

Dangessa, The Dancing Dog

Every single dark night
I come downstairs and have a fright
In the deafening silence of the room
I can just see if I loom
A dancing dog on the hob
And alright, she does a good job

Her nose is a wet blanket
Just like you'd want to drink it
She's as light as a feather
Just popped out of the nether
Friends are green and very keen

But you know what
She's my marvellous dot.

Bethany Ring (10)
Appleton Wiske CP School, Appleton Wiske

The Nestus

T iny rainbow birds
"H elp!" cried the baby bird
"E ek!" screamed the baby

N asty bird of prey
"E ek!" yelled Daddy Bird
"S it," said the big bird
"T urn, a huge bird is coming!" said the daddy bird
U nder a big patch of hair, there were a lot of eggs
S uddenly, the eggs cracked, chicks screamed.

Edward Stainthorpe (7)
Appleton Wiske CP School, Appleton Wiske

Unicorn And A Horse

- **U** inihors, small unicorn and a horse
- **I** ncredibly powerful wings on full blast... *whoosh!*
- **N** obody knows what it is unless they hear the horse of it
- **I** ncredibly hard to control its powers sometimes
- **H** orse always agile with a uni
- **O** n it is so, so fluffy
- **R** iding on it is tricky, but it is magical
- **S** o small like a rubber, but cute like a pet.

Alice King (8)
Appleton Wiske CP School, Appleton Wiske

My Pet Clumodile

My, my, it's raining cats and dogs
His fancy swimming shorts filled with lots of bogs
He loves his fashionable nails
Just like Clumodile's waving tail

How his scales shine in the sun
Making people think he has won
Crunch! goes his yellow bushy eyebrows
As huge as big circular ploughs

He is such a wonderful pet
The story shouldn't end just yet.

Katie Hutchinson (10)
Appleton Wiske CP School, Appleton Wiske

Turbo Turtle

T urbo Turtle is very, very rare
U nusual shapes on his scaly, colourful back
R eally he doesn't care
B rilliant at going as fast as a cheetah
O ut and about he likes to go

T urbo Turtle likes to race
U tterly super
R *oar!*
T urbo Turtle is a blur
L azy as a rat
E very day he is ready.

Sophie Elizabeth Green (9)
Appleton Wiske CP School, Appleton Wiske

Nocky Locky

N ocky bangs his head all the time
O *ch, ch, ch*, there goes the big brown drawer again
C lever, evil and dangerous
K *nock, knock*, goes Nocky
Y ellow nose starts to grow

L ooking slyly around
O ut of his cage, he likes to be
C ute and creamy
K angaroos are his friends
Y ellow, evil arms.

Eva Mae Pearce (7)
Appleton Wiske CP School, Appleton Wiske

Riley The Robbing Raccoon

Riley the robbing raccoon,
He's always over the moon.
When he falls from space,
He doesn't leave a trace.
Crawling into the tree,
He likes to have a cup of tea.
The cat purred,
Whilst he was a bird.
Boom! Goes the bomb,
With a gong.
He's as fluffy as fluff,
And likes to play in dandruff.
He wears a mask,
And likes to bask.

Robert Roe (8)
Appleton Wiske CP School, Appleton Wiske

Sassloth

Sassloth lives in the jungle
And she's always having a grumble
Wearing sunglasses is her thing
Like wasps' thing is, she has a sting

She is very kind
Like a fairy from mankind
She always has to be the best
Better than the rest

She's as cute as a button
but acts like a sultan
Slowly she crawls
Like a big, heavy bouncy ball.

Rosie Wilson (9)
Appleton Wiske CP School, Appleton Wiske

Caticorns

C lever, cute creatures
A dorable, little, furry body
T iny, furry paws and sparkly horn
I ndigo twirly horn
C aticorns are as small as baby unicorns
O n her head, she has a horn that looks like sweets
R un, run, Mo is on the loose. *Crash!* "We need to replant flowers."
N ever too cheeky.

Violet Rose Ellison (8)
Appleton Wiske CP School, Appleton Wiske

Hitsuna

H er ears glow in the dark and she sounds like a dog bark
I ts wings are blue and pink
T he spikes are as sharp as a knife
S he's as super as a snooper
U nder tunnels, she looks for danger
N ear danger all the time, but she's as quick as lightning
A t the end of her time, a stone was placed in her honour.

Bobby Ross (8)
Appleton Wiske CP School, Appleton Wiske

Ninja Fox

N inja Fox sleeps all day but at night he comes alive and catches the rodents
I t is as sneaky as a tiger
N inja Fox is really brave
J umping incredibly high like a kangaroo
A s he jumps around like a monkey

F urry like a bunny
O nion in his eyes, he almost cries
X -ray eyes.

Riley William Michael Jackson (10)
Appleton Wiske CP School, Appleton Wiske

Puppycorn

P uppycorn is fun and lively
U nder my bed she likes to jump
P uppycorn has a unicorn horn
P uppycorn loves me
Y ucky food it eats
C ute she is
O utside it likes to be
R ound and round it goes
"N o, no!" I say to it when it chews my new toys.

Lily Easby (7)
Appleton Wiske CP School, Appleton Wiske

Tizy

Tizy lives in a pond
He doesn't have a bond
He is very wise
And never dives. *Splash!*

As hoppy as a bunny
And he loves his honey
He is a picture
And not an itcher!

He has no friends
But his books never end
Lazily, he never gets up
Blimey, he is always in a book!

Hattie Pattison (9)
Appleton Wiske CP School, Appleton Wiske

Batcon

B ats go in caves, but not Batcon
A bove the mountains as high as a house
T iny as a rock, it flew like a bird
C loud, it went down like snow
O ver the sea and under the bridge
N orth Pole was home. Crash in the house. Goodnight and it fell asleep.

Isabelle King (8)
Appleton Wiske CP School, Appleton Wiske

Fela The Silly Monster

F ela is a three-headed monster
E yes like huge saucers
L azily he eats people
A liens' heads bright like lights
M elons he loves
E asily he eats a door
L oves to pick his nose
A ccidentally, he eats me.

Jake Graham (8)
Appleton Wiske CP School, Appleton Wiske

Crocat

C razy Crocat, a bit slimy, a bit furry
R eally likes sitting and purring
O f course he is getting into trouble
C *aboom!* He jumped into a massive puddle, *splash, splash!*
A nd I began to dash
T he end.

Poppy Race (9)
Appleton Wiske CP School, Appleton Wiske

Quad Lab

Q uad bike rider called Sam
U nlikely he will crash
A lways very cautious
D og who rides a quad

L airy as always
A lways counting sheep and cows
B ad at staying still - just wants to be on the quad!

Charlie Stainthorpe (10)
Appleton Wiske CP School, Appleton Wiske

Tom Pigeon

T om is feathery
O range eyes
M ucky and flappy

P lays music
I t can race
G reen racing pigeon
E pic
O n his feet
N asty disco pigeon.

Jack Gibson (7)
Appleton Wiske CP School, Appleton Wiske

The Tiny Tortoise

T iny as a slug
I t lives in a big log
N eon blue eyes
Y ellow feet

T im is so funny, he does funny jokes
I ncredible Tim
M ini as a twig.

Ellie McGuigan (8)
Appleton Wiske CP School, Appleton Wiske

Bob Fox

B ob Fox is very lazy
O range fur
B eady eyes

F ox eats fish
O n a night, he howls at the moon
X ylophone ribs.

Anouska Brook (7)
Appleton Wiske CP School, Appleton Wiske

Preston, The Prancing Peacock Spider

Preston's a spider like no other,
He's not scary but enjoys to bother.
Agile as a cat,
But crawls away when I try to chat.

As colourful as the rainbow,
Like something you would find in Mexico.
Four ferocious eyes,
Which he uses to catch lots of flies.

Hairy arms and legs that are long,
They are so very long.
He thinks I can't see him prancing in-between the ornaments,
Preston, this isn't a dancing tournament.

Spinning on his back, he'd breakdance away,
All of his moves put on display.
Now you know, Preston is brave and clever,
He will be your friend forever.

Anum Bashir (9)
Bantock Primary School, Penn Fields

My Kitten, Loki

Our cat, Rey, had kittens
Altogether she had three
Odin and Rune are black and white
But my favourite is Loki

He is stripy like a tiger
He likes to jump and play
He is very naughty
Almost all night and day

But sometimes he calms down
And he wants a cuddle and a pet
That is my best time with him
Loki is the cutest cat I've met.

Thalia Harris (8)
Bantock Primary School, Penn Fields

My Dog

I have a dog named Bella
Who loves to play outside
Then she starts to bark when me and Harvey hide
She runs around the garden, jumping like a flea
On the trampoline for everyone to see
When she has dinner, her eyes start to close
Now it's time for bed
She follows me upstairs
Call my mom, "Get her down!"
My bed is full of hairs!

Riley-James Proctor-Williams (8)
Bantock Primary School, Penn Fields

Iva, My Friend

My name is Iva
Hunting is my game
On the hunt I go
Don't disturb my flow
When the lid to my tank opens
Snap goes my jaw
I like fish tasting raw
I don't let it touch the floor

Iva is my friend
He may be mean
He may be lean
But Iva is my friend.

Joshua-James Bennett (8)
Bantock Primary School, Penn Fields

Dolphin Or Adventure

Dolphins, dolphins are so cute
But they are not a pet
They make the world fun
They keep people safe
They do what they are told
They make the world shine and they do it right
Because they are a dolphin, dolphin, dolphin.

Jassica Kaur (9)
Bantock Primary School, Penn Fields

Peculiar Pet

He has big horns and a red nose
He has grey fur and big soft paws
He is a wolf deer and he's big and strong
He doesn't bite at all
Because he is friendly and soft.

Catalina Bouros (9)
Bantock Primary School, Penn Fields

Scooby

I shouted for Scooby, but he wasn't there
I had looked everywhere
Then all of sudden he appeared under the chair
The next day it happened too
So I stayed with him all night long
One second he's here and the next he's gone
I couldn't find him again
All I found was a pen
Then finally, he reappeared all safe and sound
Now I'm hugging him, sitting on the ground
Randomly, I felt weird
Then noticed I had disappeared
Scooby was with me
He was all I could see
But then I was normal and then I saw Scooby too.

Kasey Humble (11)
Bedlington Station Primary School, Bedlington

Kirah's Silly Pet

B anna can walk, can talk and most of all can fly so high
A nd she has spots. When people talk to her about her spots they make her laugh
N o one can look like her, she's as tall as a tree
N obody hurts her feelings
A nna, the superhero is her best friend

C an you pick her?
O h yes, you can be her friend to the very end
R *ibbit! Ribbit!* She likes to pretend to be a frog
N ow bye!

Kirah Obrien (10)
Bedlington Station Primary School, Bedlington

The Astrocorn

You've never encountered an Astrocorn, have you?
I thought so
Well, I did!
I saw it in my dream to space
It had a pink potbelly and a rainbow mane
Her eyes shone as bright as the stars at night
She fluttered her wings like a shooting star
Astrocorn flew through the night and day
And then I shouted, "Hooray!"
If you ever go to space
Don't forget to take your camera
In case you ever encounter an Astrocorn!

Millie Barker (10)
Bedlington Station Primary School, Bedlington

The Magical Dog

A guy and his dog flying through the sky
With his big, cute puppy eyes
He said, "Go high, high, high!"
And there the dog goes, zooming through the sky
Before you knew, it turned night
But then again it turned bright
They were having too much fun
They forgot dinner or supper
Or anything other.

And that is the story of a dog and a guy
Flying through the beautiful night sky.

Nathan Leif Uddgren-Barham (10)
Bedlington Station Primary School, Bedlington

Jacko-Mantern

There he was, lurking in the night
But people see the fight in his eye
Staring to the moon
Suddenly there was a boom
Gliding over in the mist
He saw a boy with stips
There was the criminal
The threat was minimal
Case closed
The wind flows
As night, as day
He freaked away
That's the way
A hero saves the day
Hooray!

Liam Stanton (10)
Bedlington Station Primary School, Bedlington

The Kiteray

K ind and brave, Kiteray saved the day
I n the end, everyone shouted, "Hip, hip, hooray!"
T hen when the day was over, he went for a fly
E veryone said hello and goodbye
R ebecca, his mum, began to cook
A nd Kiteray got two chickens from the coop
Y ay, Kiteray saved the day.

Evie Moat (10)
Bedlington Station Primary School, Bedlington

Where Did You Go?

Donatello, what did you do?
Where are the other three fish?
We looked in the filter. No.
We looked at the bottom. No.
So does that means that Donatello ate three fish in one day?
How do we find out if he did?
We took a break and when we came back we found him dead!
And with that, two years later, we are still confused.

Ethan Loy (10)
Bedlington Station Primary School, Bedlington

My Spider Penguin

S assy
P ro at web spinning
I ndependent
D aredevil
E ven ten times cuter
R eally smart

P eculiar
E xtraordinary
N ever gives up
G ood
U ntidy
I ndestructible
N ot a bad boy.

Kolby Carrick (11)
Bedlington Station Primary School, Bedlington

Wonder Cat

Have you ever seen a cat superhero?
I saw one once, on the way back from school
It was from Planet Catopia
It had a red mask and a red cape
It had purple fur with a rainbow on it
It was fighting evil Doctor Woof
But in a marvellous flash
Evil Doctor Woof was tied up
And Wonder Cat was gone.

Harry Mason (10)
Bedlington Station Primary School, Bedlington

Giffacorn

G ood
I ncredible
F lies
F riendly
A mazing
C ute
O utstanding
R espectable
N oisy

My giffacorn can fly around at night
And sleeps through the day
She's got a big, fluffy horn
And especially big legs.

Levi Graham (10)
Bedlington Station Primary School, Bedlington

Peculiar Pogger

Have you ever seen a Pogger?
I have, every day on my morning walk
He's been there as a friend
Pogger is a mix of two pets
Half cute puppy, half slow tortoise
He has a long tail, slow feet
A loud bark like a dog, as scared as a tortoise
Pogger is my friend forever.

Josh Bell (10)
Bedlington Station Primary School, Bedlington

Dino-Dog

D ino-dog is the best
I t is fluffy and cuddly
N obody has seen it before
O range is its colour
D on't be scared, it won't bite
O nly friends it likes to make
G reen spokes go down its back to its tail.

Aiden Falloon (10)
Bedlington Station Primary School, Bedlington

Octo-Seal

The other day I saw an Octo-Seal
It was eating a wheel
That's a weird meal
Maybe it was unwell
I couldn't tell
If it would even sell
Would it ring a bell?
If it did I would yell
I would say...
Hooray!

Charlie Ullock (10)
Bedlington Station Primary School, Bedlington

Hammy The Hero!

H e saves the world every night
A ll the villains are left in a fright
M ay I mention his mech-rider
M aybe he's cute, but he's a good fighter
Y ou are the best, Hammy the hamster!

Dean Foster (10)
Bedlington Station Primary School, Bedlington

Vampire-Corn-Wolf

B eastly
E vil
L egendary rare
L egendary skills
A nd if you make it angry, it will suck your blood

S trong
W ild
A lways wanted
N asty.

Phoebe Macneish (10)
Bedlington Station Primary School, Bedlington

Gibbs

G ibbs is a special bird
I t works for the RAF
B eautiful and cuddly, yes it is
B ut it's not a force to be reckoned with
S o, if you are an enemy, try not to fight with Gibbs.

Jack Simpson (10)
Bedlington Station Primary School, Bedlington

Coco The Astronaut

The other day I adopted a hamster
She was so adorable and cute
Every night she sits straight
And *whoosh!* off she goes
Flying as high as the moon!

Hallie Taylor (10)
Bedlington Station Primary School, Bedlington

Powerful Polly

Who needs muddling maps
Or time to learn misty magic tricks
When you have a majestic magic horn
It gloriously glows in rippling rainbow
My pet's name is Polly
With a picture-perfect smile
And eagle-eyed vision
Her horn has phenomenal powers
She always leaps over leopard toys
She is my powerful pet.

Shanzeh Khan (7)
Cale Green Primary School, Shaw Heath

Swirly

S wirly is my pet's name
W hat he does is try to fly
I nside or out, it's all the same
R ocketing across the sky
L ook at him go!
Y ou'll love him too, I know!

Tilly Lee (7)
Cale Green Primary School, Shaw Heath

My Dancing Hamster, Bubblegum

B ounce around the floor
U pwards to the sky
B eat to the music
B alance on one foot
L anding on two feet
E xcited to dance
G reat at spinning on his head
U nder the bridge, he dances
M usic he dances to all day.

A M (8)
Chase House School, Brownhills

Smoky The Cat

Smoky the cat
Loved to rap
Never miaows
But sings
Plays in the park
Plays in the dark
Plays on all the swings.

Beau Reading (8)
Chase House School, Brownhills

Elina The Cabbit

I was at a swimming pool one day
When a weird swimming animal came to say hey
I asked her what was going on
She told me she'd been there since dawn
I told her that I had to go home
I found out then she had a heart of stone
She fought a bird that pooped on my head
She told me she'd protect me until I was dead
I asked her what her name was and she said it was Elina
She had the head of a cat and the body of a rabbit
Her tail was as long as Route 66
Elina's eyes were like sapphires
Her fur was ginger
Sometimes she was a bit of a whinger
But it's okay because she's a very peculiar pet.

Eve Millar (11)
Hillington Primary School, Hillington

The Extraordinary Eagle

One very playful day, I went out to play
I saw an eagle flying high, then I shouted, "Hi!"
The eagle flew down to me and picked me up
Then me and the eagle were soaring through the big blue sky
Then I realised when we were about to land
The eagle's beak was gold like sand
Before the eagle was about to leave, I called her Elise
I think she liked it because she was jumping up and down
But she then had an awful frown
Elise then started to sob, I gave her some corn on the cob
She felt better and then the weather turned to a storm
Me and Elise flew high in the sky
We saw every single special sight.

Abigail Sarah McMahon (10)
Hillington Primary School, Hillington

Wart The Worm

Wart was an extraordinary worm
He could get away from birds if he wiggled and squirmed
You may ask, why's he in the sky?
He has wings, so he could fly
This is his tale, we won't go too far
Read along, but don't get stuck in a jar!
Wart was in his car, going to school
But what he wanted to do was chill in his pool
So he flew away, up so high
Up above the clouds, up in the sky
Wart flew home and went down
He went to his owner, who looked at him with a frown
Wart looked up at his owner, who looked pretty old
His owner saw Wart poop gold!
And therefore, his extraordinary tale was told.

Dylan Burns (12)
Hillington Primary School, Hillington

My Special Burtle, Bob!

I have a very special pet burtle
One night, when I couldn't sleep
I found my burtle flying away out my window
I found out that my burtle heads to Kurtel every night
An hour before he left one night
I leapt on his back and enjoyed the ride
When we arrived, I was very surprised
It was filled with stuff of every colour
Red, orange, yellow, green, blue, pink, purple
The only bad part was I had to go home
Since I couldn't keep my eyes open
As I was as sleepy as a sloth
No matter how old I will be
I will never forget that night
My burtle took me to Kurtel!

Lucy McLean (11)
Hillington Primary School, Hillington

The Snail Who Lost His Sass

Sheldon was in an animal shelter
A person came in to buy him
But even though he was quick, he got bought
He tried to get out, pushing, grunting...
It didn't work, he was trapped
When he got home, he was in a cage
Yes, a cage, a snail in a cage
Mind you, this was not an ordinary snail
He was none other than Sassy Snail
He was slick
He had a motto: 'The Slick and Sassy Snail!'
One day, the owner took Sheldon out of his cage
And told him a nice long story
It had a lot of characters and he lost his sass.
It's okay, he was nice, calm and relaxed.

Rhiannon McFadden (10)
Hillington Primary School, Hillington

The Fox Bandit

Once there was a fox who really liked to steal
Obviously, people would find it, so he hid in a field
Once he wanted something more, something bigger
So he decided to steal a chest
When it was night-time, he really tried his best
He snuck and crept, grabbed it with his paw while everybody slept
He snuck out of the house as quiet as a mouse
Once he had headed out, it was like he'd won a joust
Then once morning struck, he was really hoping he had good luck,
But it turned out it had a tracking device
He was kicked out of the village and called a Little Mice.

Aston Daly (10)
Hillington Primary School, Hillington

Flora The Flexy Flamingo

   F unny to be with but be on her good side
   L et her entertain you with her flexibility
   E xtraordinarily charming but naughty
e **X** tra organised like a squirrel
   Y es is always her answer

   F lat at times because she is so bendy
   L ipstick is her essential need
   A s flexible as string but as hard as nails
   M indful (most of the time)
   I ncredibly inspirational
   N ever cold in her life
   G ood at gymnastics
   O bedient to her parents.

Isha Zaheer (10)
Hillington Primary School, Hillington

Andy And Me

Only at night, my fish glows up bright
When midnight comes, she grows up giant
She grows arms and legs and has a little tiny egg
She is going to be a mum
So we ran to the sea to go for our last swim
But she didn't feel good so she rested in my hood
And fell right asleep
Then she was a small fish again
I ran down to the shore
And then we were home again
I put her in her tank and lay down to rest
At four o'clock dead, baby fish were swimming about
When I looked for my fish, she lay there dead.

Maisie McLaughlin (10)
Hillington Primary School, Hillington

Plen The Pengocrog

Pleng the pengocrog is a very weird pet
Probably one you have never met
With the ears of a dog
Head of a crocodile and the bottom of a penguin
But overall, I think he gets to win
Because he is a very weird thing
Also, guess what? He can sing
But it's very hard because of his teeth as sharp as a sword
It was as loud as a foghorn
But was fine after he had some corn
That's his favourite, you have probably guessed
He is my little pest
Pleng the pengocrog.

Aaliyah Sinclair (11)
Hillington Primary School, Hillington

My Silly Spragon

S ibbel the spragon lives in a wagon
P ompom the dog next door screams and scratches to see Sibbel on the other side of her door!
R *oar!* Sibbel shouts to see Pompom behind her door
A spider crossed with a dragon, that's what a spragon is
G rowls can be heard from my spragon's wagon when she sleeps
O n her tail, I sit when we go fly at midnight
N ot one, but three wardrobes for my amazing silly big spragon, Sibbel.

Alexa Ingram (11)
Hillington Primary School, Hillington

Lee, The Lizard Princess

I have a lizard princess, oh yes, he's very pretty
He prances and dances all night long
He loves to sing a little song to get me out of bed
His name is Lee, he's from Dundee
And he adores afternoon tea
He has a crown as shiny as the stars
Oh yes, he is very rich, he owns seven cars
He is, in fact, a pretty princess
As pretty as the sea
He is, in fact, a pretty princess
Almost as pretty as me!

Kayla Mullin (10)
Hillington Primary School, Hillington

Flying Dogs?

I have a dog named Snow
Who has been acting kinda, I don't know...
Kinda off lately
So I took her to the vet
And they told me I have a flying pet!
Ever since that day
I've been thinking she is crazy
But one night she took me on a ride
And she bought her friends along
She said it's where she belonged
It was a hard decision but I had to let her go
And said goodbye and off she went.

Rebecca Burns (9)
Hillington Primary School, Hillington

George The Gelephant

G eorge the gelephant is a mix between a gerbil and an elephant
E xtraordinary giant ears sit on the head of George
L egs as short as tiny, broken sticks
E legant like a ballerina
P rances around the room in his hamster ball
H is trunk is as long as a snake
A nd his eyes are as cute as buttons
N igel is his owner's name
T iny like a mouse.

Myley McFlynn (11)
Hillington Primary School, Hillington

The Nerdy Pug

An adorable pug, the eyes glow like the moon with the stars in the night sky
In the day something magical happens.
Like no other, she starts to learn word by word
She gets smarter and smarter.
Day by day, the smartest animal is here to stay
One day, Sally said, "Oh no! There is no more learning to do."
She tries to speak but nothing comes out and the little dog shed a tear.

Liam Elliot (9)
Hillington Primary School, Hillington

Sidney, The Sassy Spider

One day, I went to the shops to get a pet
I found a spider
It had a black leather jacket, pink nails and ripped black jeans
And red lipstick, it was called Sidney
We brought her, but she will never open her eyes
Because she thought it was sassy!
So we tried to open her eyes, but she bit us!
Luckily we dodged it
We returned her because she bites!

Aidan Lindsay (10)
Hillington Primary School, Hillington

Layla, The Skateboarding Lizard

Layla, the skateboarding lizard, is my ferocious pet
She has black beady eyes, three of them
Her skin is as green as an emerald
On the way home from Lizard School
Layla had her skateboard, so she skated home
On the way home, Layla landed her first ollie,
Layla did such a high ollie she saw space!
The moon was as bright as a light.

Ellie Rae Stewart (11)
Hillington Primary School, Hillington

Mango, The Marvellous Monkey

This is the greatest monkey you will ever see
And when he was only two years of age
He learned to stand up and pee
He's balanced on sticks
He's balanced on chairs
He's balanced on a lot of things
But his next task is a bear
He's as fast as lightning
And that is the marvellous monkey.

Jack Sherriff (10)
Hillington Primary School, Hillington

Pekky Pig

P ekky hates people
E nough for her heart to be stone-cold
K henzo is her only friend
K henzo is a kangaroo
Y ellow is Pekky's favourite colour

P ekky is a magic pig, deep
I nto the night she will dance around in my clothes
G oodness me!

Stephen Smith (10)
Hillington Primary School, Hillington

Cat With A Hat

A hat on a cat
How about that?
A cat that can tell
With a shell
This cat is as fat as a hippo
Again with that hat
This cat has a hat
A top hat
This cat can shrink
And become pink
This cat can't tell
When it's in its shell
But out of the shell
It can tell.

Lewis Brown (11)
Hillington Primary School, Hillington

Fuzzy, The Freaky Rat

Fuzzy the rat is very fat
He likes to eat
He also likes to play on a mat
Fuzzy has eyes as grey as a dark cloud
And very loud
He has got very weak feet
But he is very proud
Fuzzy is messy
And not as nice as his friend, Jessy
During the night
He always gets a fright.

Hollie Kinnear (11)
Hillington Primary School, Hillington

The Lazy Rabbit

Sits all day, gets takeaways all night
This lazy rabbit never wants to fight
Watches 'Stranger Things'
And other programmes that zing
Tiny but whiny
This rabbit gets her way
Fur as soft as a cloud and a wee bit loud
Kiwi, the lazy rabbit, makes me proud.

Mirren McGregor (10)
Hillington Primary School, Hillington

The Monkey With The Amazing Syle

Princess Pop is a beautiful monkey
She wears a flowy pink tutu
With white and pink striped ballet shoes
She also wears a crown that is as shiny as gold
Princess Pop wears her tutu every day
Because it gives her powers
Her power is to make people happy.

Brooke Lipsett (11)
Hillington Primary School, Hillington

Snerret's Secret

S mall as a mouse
N ever eats
E veryone's afraid
R oads are quiet
R ight outside
E verywhere he does magic
T omorrow is an adventure.

Brooke Lang (10)
Hillington Primary School, Hillington

The Escaping Mittens

The mittens escaped from the kittens
The kittens were looking for the mittens
The mittens got lost
The kittens were as sad as a blue whale
The mittens were as happy as a dancing bear.

Ava Brown (10)
Hillington Primary School, Hillington

Beagle

Bingo the beagle
Long as a log
Walks like an eagle
He's a long dog

Bingo loves his walks
He shakes and shakes
He barks when he talks
When he swims in a lake

He takes up the bus
Off to London
Sees his friend, Mass
But he goes to Huntingdon

Off we go
On the underground
I saw something though
Now I hear a sound
Oh no, I've been found
Does he mean harm?
But there's no one around
There's a face appearing from the farm

Now I'm back home
I'm going to sleep
I'm off to bed
I landed in a heap
I'm Bingo the beagle!

Owen Vinton (9)
Holme CE Primary Academy, Holme

The Magic Baarpet

I got home from school the other day
And I heard a "Bah!" down the hallway
I walked into the living room to sit on the carpet
That we bought yesterday at the supermarket
It started to vibrate at ten at night
I almost fell off as it took off in flight
We crashed through the ceiling and zoomed through the sky
I heard it "Bah!" and thought, *that's why!*
It grew a head on its rear, the fur started to shear
It was starting to disappear, so I said
"Oh dear!"

Jessica Hume (9)
Holme CE Primary Academy, Holme

Cat Fish Called Dave

I couldn't sleep all night
Because I had a fright
Where I was at the highest height
but I guess I did like the sight

When I woke up I screamed a big scream
Because I had the weirdest dream
My cat went down a slide and said, "Weee!"
When he came back down, I said, "Come and get clean!"

My cat has a fish tail
The water park sent me a letter in the mail
It said I had a fine, then I let out a wail
Why does my cat have a fish tail?

Loretta Davis (9)
Holme CE Primary Academy, Holme

My Devilish Dog

My dog's name is Leo
And don't mistake it for Theo
As he chews sticks and stones
And could easily break your bones!

One day, a baby grabbed his tail
And that really made him wail
So he turned around to give a bite
And he gave the baby such a fright

One time I picked him up
He wriggled and made me drop my cup
Soon it hit the ground with a smash
And one bit hit my mum's eyelash!

Ben Leschallas (10)
Holme CE Primary Academy, Holme

Xander The Panda

I have a pet panda
Whose name is Xander
Who loves bamboo
Who produces a lot of poo

I know this sounds crazy
He likes to drink gravy
At midnight one night
I saw my panda take flight

He flew to the mountain
Where there was a fountain
With lots of bamboo
So he lived there, my panda, Xander.

Bella Marshall (9)
Holme CE Primary Academy, Holme

The Cats Who Fight And Bite

This cat is so tame
Captain Snugglepants is his name
He has a sister
Man, she's sinister
At night they are a fright
At 11am they'll party on you
Man, that leaves a bruise
So treat them right
Or they'll bite
And fight all night.

Noah Weston (10)
Holme CE Primary Academy, Holme

The Catfish

I was fishing in the lake
Waiting for a cake to bake
I saw a cat in the water
So I got the net and caught her
I flipped her over and saw a fin
So I chucked her in the bin
I wondered about this peculiar creature
And her crazy feature.

Ben Oliver Burks (10)
Holme CE Primary Academy, Holme

Lion Cheetah

My lion, called Zion, has wings and eats chocolate kings
He can breathe underwater, its prey it slaughters
His body is yellow and spotted black
He has an orange mane, with a yellow back and a small face
His prey he chases.

Zion Mugabo (10)
Holme CE Primary Academy, Holme

The Cute Cat

There is a cat that flies
Lives in New York
Every day, the cat
Called Daniel, flies

Where he goes
Is unknown
He's just a cat
He has a sister
She is ten years older
Than Dan.

Harry Chapman (10)
Holme CE Primary Academy, Holme

Gigigula

Shy and deadly
Still and steady
In the night he creeps and crawls
Until the time is right to brawl
It's trainer stood beside it
When it's fainted, it goes back
Then it must be avenged.

Dylan Stevenson (9)
Holme CE Primary Academy, Holme

My Turtle, Fred

My turtle, Fred
He is not dead
But when he does die
I guess he'll fly

And when he flies
I'll say goodbye
To my turtle, Fred
Who may be dead.

Noah Dyball (10)
Holme CE Primary Academy, Holme

There's A Fox In A Box

I woke up at night
And shivered in fright
After I saw a peculiar sight
A fluffy fox
Sleeping in a box
Covered in a sleeping bag, wearing socks.

Keeley Welch (10)
Holme CE Primary Academy, Holme

Pickle!
A kennings poem

Treat-guzzler
Loud-purrer
Food-stealer
Shadow-chaser
Nerve-tangler
Clumsy-climber
Grumpy-groaner
Fur-patchworker
Wiry whiskers.

Vito Max Wolsing (10)
Holme CE Primary Academy, Holme

The Dog In The Lamp

There once was a dog who lived in a lamp
Excitedly, he popped out
But no one believed he could grant wishes
So he was shoved back in again!

Eli Colam (10)
Holme CE Primary Academy, Holme

The Dog

He is a dog
He's like a frog
He bounces around
Like a clown

He's like a mop
He likes to lick flip flops.

Ayden Pattison (10)
Holme CE Primary Academy, Holme

Jam Jam

Jam Jam is small
He lives in my pocket
My pocket is like a rocket
My pocket is nice
My pocket is snug in a bug.

Elie Connell (10)
Holme CE Primary Academy, Holme

Peculiar Pet, Sosule

S assy, nasty attitude when woken from deep sleep
O nly eats vegetables and meat, it will refuse anything else, such as sugar and dairy
S kin is gold and scaly, though it's not very scary
U niquely smart and is always happy
L ovely with children and can jump amazingly high
E ats all the time if it's allowed and loves looking at the sky.

Riley Stobbs (9)
Johnson Fold Community Primary School, Bolton

Dogcat

Dogcat is the cutest animal of them all
He's furry and has nice dark eyes
He's colourful and oh so cute and clever and he's quite long
Here's a warning, be careful of his teeth
They're sharper than a chainsaw
And be careful of the wild ones
The dog's face is black
And the cat's face is ginger.

Harrison Bond (9)
Johnson Fold Community Primary School, Bolton

The Ferocious, Big Tigolf The Wolf

A tiger and a wolf is a big, fascinating, ferocious tigolf
With sharp, big and furious teeth
And it's super, super fast
So fast, it's able to go to the past
It has big red and black eyes
With a long, scruffy and fluffy tail
He can do a lot of things wrong
But he is very, very strong.

Charlie Greenhalgh (9)
Johnson Fold Community Primary School, Bolton

Sharkion

S uper colossal body
H appy moods
A nd always smiles
R ed, cute crystal eyes
K ind-natured if somebody's injured
I s also super cute
O nly like eating vegetables
N ormally naughty natured.

Athena Mckenzie (9)
Johnson Fold Community Primary School, Bolton

Peculiar Pet Snurtle

S o clever, adorable, has no friends
N umber one pet not to buy, trust me!
U nkind and evil to everyone
R ough and scratches people
T errible pet to feed
L oves food but bites
E xtreme pet.

Katie Newton (10)
Johnson Fold Community Primary School, Bolton

Spowl

My pet is very scary
Its legs are long and hairy
His beak is pink and wide
To eat you up alive
And if you really dare
To go to his lair
He won't bear
To put you in despair!

Lily Pennington (9)
Johnson Fold Community Primary School, Bolton

Koatig

K illing massive claws
O range, long stripes
A dorable puppy eyes
T ough muscly body
I ncredible long tail
G entle, sensitive nose.

Chloe Louise Gregson (9)
Johnson Fold Community Primary School, Bolton

Mercat

M arvellous swooshing tail
E yes of sky-blue
R ound, slimy
C olourful scales
A nd soft furry ears
T otally peculiar pet.

Faye Bourke, Rach & Tomasz Sadzik (9)
Johnson Fold Community Primary School, Bolton

Eliger

A haiku

Eliger is old
He is also very cold
He is hard to hold.

Kacie Smith (10)
Johnson Fold Community Primary School, Bolton

Caramel, The Colour-Changing Parrot

I have a pet parrot
She likes to eat carrots
She creeps about at night to have a little bite
She is wild and messy and changes colour too
She likes to have a party
She parties all night too
In the day, she acts like a normal parrot
But at night it's time to rock the night
At night, that's when Caramel changes
From purple to blue to pink
She's scared in case people find out
She walks around about
At night, she flies out and flies with the clouds
She makes figures with the clouds
And plays hide-and-seek
Sometimes she hides too well
She can never seek
She is sometimes lonely and has nothing to do
But when it's night-time, she has loads of fun too!

Amy Robbins (10)
Mill Of Mains Primary School, Dundee

The Speedy Sloth

Sloths are very slow
Sloths are very clever
But this peculiar sloth is speedy like ever
He is sassy and fun
When the sky is dark and the moon is high
This peculiar sloth races through the night
In the day, this speedy sloth
Is the same as all the others
They don't know about his peculiar skill
On weekdays, there are races
For cheetahs, rabbits and pumas
The speedy sloth wants a go
But I don't think so
The sloth was bored one the day
He runs away, but not for long
After a while, he comes back home
He loves to run, he loves to race
But one day, it's not so great.

Lacey Stewart (10)
Mill Of Mains Primary School, Dundee

The Breakdancing Turtle

Blitz is my peculiar pet
Late at night, he begins to rehearse for his shows
"Tortoises don't breakdance!" people say
Zero people go to his shows
The other animals started to
He cannot live without breakdancing
Elliot is his best friend
The shows are put on TV
Oh, I love the shows he puts on
Rosco is the stage manager who helps in Blitz's shows
Taking glory he likes
On and off, the stage lights
I am proud of my peculiar pet
Shows are one of Blitz's favourite things
Every animal that sees him thinks he's the best

Qais Naseer (11)
Mill Of Mains Primary School, Dundee

Dock, The Sausage Dog/Duck

Dock is a very cute dog/duck
During the day, Dock is brown
At night, he glows up and changes colours
He glows so brightly, it nearly blinds you
He is dangerous to some people
I don't think he is dangerous
He loves me so much
He can even eat with a fork or spoon
I like playing ball with him
After we play ball, he is tired
I take him to meet his girlfriend at the park
He walks strangely with his dog/duck legs
That is everything about Dock.

Lacey Murphy (9)
Mill Of Mains Primary School, Dundee

Emerald The Unique Dolphin

Emerald is a unique dolphin
She likes to swim and play
She hides away from everyone
And hides beneath the caves
She always plays by herself
And always swims alone
She's afraid that she will be exposed
And worse, not feel at home
She tries to keep her abilities in control
For when she gets too sad
She would make the ground quake
And feel ever so bad
Every teardrop from her eye
Looks like a rainbow in the sky.

Aimie Milne (10)
Mill Of Mains Primary School, Dundee

Flying Nayla

F lying through the sky
L ittle Nayla goes
Y outhful and graceful
I climbed onto Nayla's back and we flew up
N ight-night little Nayla
G oes up in the night

N ayla is so sassy
A bout that day, she found a friend
Y ou'll always be my little Nayla
L ittle Nayla zooms through the night
A s she does tricks.

Alix Sutherland (10)
Mill Of Mains Primary School, Dundee

The Ice Skating Turtle

Turtles are really lazy and slow
Turtles are very messy and cute
But this particular turtle is very funny and clever
He can twirl on ice
He is really sassy and wild
He's adorable and noisy
When the sky is dark, his back glows green
He is very colourful
Skating around the ice
In the middle of the night
He outshines the moon
On the rink of the ice.

Madison Adams (9)
Mill Of Mains Primary School, Dundee

Little Timmy

L ittle Timmy is the best pet in the world
I love him so much
T immy is what I call him for short
T immy is a ninja monkey
L ike his mum and dad and
E llie, his wife

T immy is no ordinary pet
I might tell my mum
M y mum now knows
M y dad now knows
Y ou do as well.

Callum Carson (9)
Mill Of Mains Primary School, Dundee

Blitz, The Super Raccoon

My peculiar pet is a raccoon
Not just any raccoon, but a super raccoon
His name is Blitz
He loves to play all day
But when it's night, he's up for a fight
He loves tickles on his belly
His paws are black like super gloves
He has a red face mark that looks like a mask
He is a little naughty, but I still love him so much!

Mylah Dodds-Jackson (10)
Mill Of Mains Primary School, Dundee

Rappa Jagga

R appa Jagga is his name
A cool guy he is
P ut his Lamborghini in the shed
P ut his diamond chain above his bed
A nice voice he has

J agga is what I call him for short
A n amazing mansion he has
G reat for parties
G reat for pets
A nd he is my friend.

Ava Egan (10)
Mill Of Mains Primary School, Dundee

Brownie The Sloth

I have a pet sloth
She likes to eat moths
She likes to play and jog
And she likes to follow a hedgehog
She's lazy and clever
But she's an incredible thing

She likes to play songs all night long
And dance to songs
Her sisters join in
She likes them to join her
And that's my rhyme done!

Autumn Iannetta (10)
Mill Of Mains Primary School, Dundee

Koko The Kung-Fu Koala

Koko is one dangerous koala
He can even fight an iguana
Even though he mostly hangs in trees
He even likes to play with bees
Koko can speak in Japanese
But his favourite thing of all is to train with me
His cosy bed is high up in the trees
It's Koko's bedtime now
So I probably have to tuck him in now.

Brèagha Stewart (9)
Mill Of Mains Primary School, Dundee

My Pet Bunny, Zachary

My pet bunny, Zachary, is very peculiar
He is an engineer
He is always jumping
On Friday, when we go to the skip
That's where he gets his parts
He's scared of heights
He has blue fur
Today I was starving
So I bit into a carrot and almost lost a tooth!
It was my bunny's screwdriver!

Noah Snee (10)
Mill Of Mains Primary School, Dundee

Ants

My peculiar pets are singing insects
More specifically, they're ants
They're that good, they have their own pants
Although their pay is quite small
A long time ago, at the mall
They were doing a show
That was when they took a big blow
They packed their bags, shouting, "Go!"

Rosco McBride (10)
Mill Of Mains Primary School, Dundee

Miami, The Mini-Sized Llama

Miami is a mini-sized llama
She has bright blue eyes
And nice white fluffy hair
Miami is funny and feisty
She's cute and kind
I take her everywhere with me
Sometimes people are scared of her
But I'm not
My mini llama is just the best.

Mylie Watt (10)
Mill Of Mains Primary School, Dundee

Business Monkey

My monkey is a businessman
His office is a bathroom

His name is Bob
He likes to drive a Lamborghini
If I'm good he'll give me a ride

I hope I get a fancy car
But he's probably going to buy
The fancy things for himself.

Ollie Sime (9)
Mill Of Mains Primary School, Dundee

Pando

P andas sit and eat bamboo, but Pando doesn't
A ll watch as Pando balances on his head
N o one knows how, he just stays upside down
D oes he see any other animals in the forest?
O ther animals don't get how he can do it.

Lenny Christie (10)
Mill Of Mains Primary School, Dundee

The Ice Skating Elephant

Ellie lives at the ice rink
Once I took her to a lesson
Ellie curved and curved all around
She ate pizzas and ice cream
She could dance on the ice too
Ellie made a friend, her name was Nayla the elephant
She finally left the ice rink today.

Elly-May Mann (10)
Mill Of Mains Primary School, Dundee

King Cloud

We bought a panda
His name is King Cloud
He is as white as a cloud
At night, he glows outside
He is ready to fly in the sky
In the day, he's not so great
In the morning, he is very dull
You hardly see him.

Logan Smith (10)
Mill Of Mains Primary School, Dundee

Coffee Connoisseur

Corey the cat is a coffee connoisseur
Bakes his own beans and grinds them till they're pure
Espresso, latte and Americano
The baristas are all happy
Because they get to take some home.

Harry Scott (10)
Mill Of Mains Primary School, Dundee

Hugo, The Robo Dog

H ugo is my peculiar pet
U nbelievably fast he is at running
G igantic and cool
O cean coloured, he is really bright.

Jude Ferrie (10)
Mill Of Mains Primary School, Dundee

Mertle The Turtle With A Meercat Body

M ighty, magnificent Mertle is a mix of a meerkat and a turtle. This creature will hurt you with their eyes.
E ven if you are nice to this creature, you are still dead. These creatures are very rare to find and they have the senses of a shark
R ed is blood, blood is dead. I'd run if I were you. This creature will kill you and feast on you
T he massive, beady black eyes, oh how powerful they are, always protecting their babies so nobody can take them
L ovely on the outside, but trust me, not on the inside, they're so eager to get food
E very single day, a new baby is born. Monkeys like to eat them, so the parents always make them run.

Rafael Corona (9)
St Mary's RC Primary School, Swinton

My Best Friend, The Tyranna-Walrus-Rex

I have a Tyranna-Walrus-Rex, he's my pet, yes my pet
But he's too big to be true and messy and he's scared of the vet
He's not that gentle but he doesn't mean to be
It's an endangered species and he just wants to be free
Usually, he's grumpy like he was today
He costs a lot so you need a good pay

It has little, stubby green and red claws
And usually he does these very weird roars
But when the sun goes down
He starts to frown
When the sun comes up, it makes his day bright
Because he's so ferocious, he scares the neighbour's pup

He eats in the bin and once he found a shark fin
It lives in the shed but doesn't like to go in
And it robs the butchers for normal food

Most of the time most certainly rude
He's not that cunning
But he's at the very peak at running

He's my best friend in all the world
But one time he nicked my mum's necklace made of pearls
He flies up in the evening to say goodnight
He's my pet and he always will be
But there's one problem, he looks like me.

Jack Burton (10)
St Mary's RC Primary School, Swinton

Owlcta

Outstanding Owlcta is a cute creature
Especially if you count every one of its features
First, is its humongous owl head
If you're wondering, it's even bigger than 100 pieces of lead
She lives in a cave
Not in a grave

This is a very rare creature with tiny yellow cat legs
They're about the same size as ten red pegs
From a distance, if you can see its head, which is pink
It's even brighter than a shiny kitchen sink
On top of Mount Everest
Which is like a huge dinner guest

She has a black owl tail
It wouldn't even blend in the snow
Its body is lime-green
Which matches its personality, which is mean
It has cat ears
Which have been there for years

It also has a red cat tail
Even though it is a female
Orange, spiky wings which it has
Even though it never goes to pass
Candy which she eats regrows off her head
Not delicious raw red meat.

Olivia Seddon (10)
St Mary's RC Primary School, Swinton

Pekko The Peculiar

Pekko is my pet parrot, but he is very strange
He can see from a far range
He has the bottom and abilities of a gekko
And that is the reason I call him Pekko
He is adorable in every way
But if you imagine him, you will pay
This parrot isn't an ordinary bird
As soon as you see him, you will be lured
One day you will see him awake
Or you can see him asleep or near the lake
Pekko has many marvellous skills
Like camouflage and flying over hills
Do not dare touch his colourful wings
Or it will be the opposite of how it sings
Pekko is my pet
And don't catch him in a net!

Oscar Tomlinson (9)
St Mary's RC Primary School, Swinton

The Chicken Ogre

C hicken ogres are very rare
H ow rare you say, just like a hare
I f you go near it, that's the wrong choice
C hicken ogres will take your voice
K icking, pushing, pulling you around
E ven in the night, you will have a surround
N o one will survive the chicken ogres

O gres are scary and chickens are loners
G o home and lock the door
R un away and wish it never happened before
E ven in the night, they're coming for you and if you tell your family, they won't ignore you...

Ellana Fahy (9)
St Mary's RC Primary School, Swinton

Howlines

My peculiar pet is an odd one indeed
On veggies, meat and you, it will feed
Its fur is the perfect grey
Just like a rainy day

They will chew on your bones
Whilst I put down the cones
Just to keep you away
You would be a fool to stay

They have lots of powers, each a different one
But if they start to use them, you might want to run
Fire, ice, water, breeze, their powers are all of these
Nature is the rarest
Stay away please

Other than that, they're amazing pets with ten lives
They go by the name Howlines.

Maisie-Rae Foster (9)
St Mary's RC Primary School, Swinton

The Catadactyl

C atadactyl is a very lazy animal, it sleeps all day and all night
A catadactyl is scary and will hurt you
T asting every water drop, he will hear you in the dark
A catadactyl has very big claws and is very tall
D ark is when the catadactyl comes out with a shout
A ll animals fear the big catadactyl especially all fish
C arrying all the meat in sight
T aller than a skyscraper, it gives a shout
Y es, it even has electric prickles down its back
L iving in the jungle it has a bad smell.

Annie McKiernan (10)
St Mary's RC Primary School, Swinton

The Squiraffe

S quiraffe sprinting round all the trees in the jungle
Q uietly hunting its unexpecting prey
U ncomfortingly glaring right at you
I would run, scream and cry for help, but nothing would work, it would end you before you start to hurt
R unning in a blur, stomping on the ground, somehow making no sound
A ware that its bite will put you in shock
F rom sunrise to sunset, this beast is hunting you down
F ighting back, run away before he gives you a fright
E nding the life of everything in sight.

Nathan Rolfe (10)
St Mary's RC Primary School, Swinton

A Catchkin

You must be aware of a catchkin
It has sharp teeth to eat chicken nuggets with
It's lazy but very fast
No matter what you do
Do not stroke it or it will bite your fingers
The catchkin is extinct and wants to be free
Do not go to a catchkin's hut for tea
Or you'll be turned into a pea
The catchkin can only speak at night
So be aware you might get a fright
A catchkin loves to watch movies
And blends dogs tails for smoothies
Everyone is scared of the catchkin
The catchkin thought that everyone cared.

Orla Bramble (9)
St Mary's RC Primary School, Swinton

Emotion Dog

E ach emotion dog lives in Salford, well unless they're a stray
M ost emotion dogs chew on human bones
O r on human skin
T hey want to take over the world
I wanted one myself, but my mum told me this
O n the hills, they hide and then strike at night
N o one sees them, they are light brown but they are a fright

D ay or night, they don't care, they will eat you without a doubt
O h, and they can speak
G eorge, it is me and I'm one of them.

George Kinman (9)
St Mary's RC Primary School, Swinton

The Turtlion

Fighting through the fields
Is the turtlion which peels of its prey's skin
With its razor-sharp teeth
Never stare this creature in its laser eyes

This creepy creature eats a handful of humans
As soon as this monster meets its prey, *boom!* it's dead
This weird creature loves clay
The turtlion cuddles and snuggles with its dead prey

This deadly creature lives in dark, creepy caves
The people that go there get sleepy and pass out
These creatures live for a creepy 10,000 years.

Jake Bird (9)
St Mary's RC Primary School, Swinton

Stigasaurus

S tigasaurus flying through the sky
T iny stigasaurus, wandering through the sky
I f you stare into its eyes, it will kill you
G enius stigasaurus, munching people up
A hill, a big tall tree that's all it needs
S tigasaurus walking on earth
A lso, outside earth is its home
U nder the stars it lives on the moon
R unning on the moon like a daft fool
U p and around the earth
S tigasaurus flying through the sky.

Alfie Fanning (9)
St Mary's RC Primary School, Swinton

Klaus The Catadactyl

Klaus the catadactyl, the strangest animal alive today
His wings are waving and goes up, up and away
The head of a Bombay, but the razor-sharp feet of a pterodactyl
Every night, when we go to bed, he needs a hat full of people to eat

Although he is scared of the vet
I almost cried when we met
We met on a hilltop
Where he spilt my bottle of pop

At times he could be nice
He will eat your mice
He lives in a cave
People say I'm brave.

Poppy Fletcher (10)
St Mary's RC Primary School, Swinton

Pog!

Here comes the pog
Biting and poking and biting through animals, killing everything
His razor-sharp teeth and claws biting through your body
Stabbing your heart and using it for its desert
Whilst using its napkin as it's your own skin
If a pog sees you, make sure you say your last words
Whilst he flies up and drops on your head
You will never escape the pog!
Be scared if you don't know where he lives
The forest, there's so many, so run!

Alex Kavanagh (9)
St Mary's RC Primary School, Swinton

The Scarefish

S leeping in the coral, Zanzo-Cleo awakes
C an't stop screaming, what loud noise he makes!
A riana Grande is his favourite singer
R ings and lipstick is his special ability
E ar-bleeding screams are always heard
F aces are full of agony when they cross this fish
I ndeed, he could kill anyone with his yells
S creaming and shouting are always his routine
H e is really scared of water. No surprise!

Sophie Fountain (9)
St Mary's RC Primary School, Swinton

Shadow, The D.A.C.

S hadow is a wonder, she really is the best cat
H er coat is as black as the night sky and at twilight she becomes D.A.C.
A round midnight, she transforms and sprouts her angel wings and halo, don't forget her devil tail
D .A.Cs are so very rare, there's only six left in the whole universe, oh, and she's from Mars
O h, at night, how fast she flies
W ow, Devil Angel Cats are the best and I love them.

Rebekah Coates (9)
St Mary's RC Primary School, Swinton

Midnight The Horse

M idnight the magical winged horse
I n the starry and misty night
D ancing, playing and skipping with me
N ow that the moon's glowing beautifully bright
I 'm now riding her back on her gorgeous brown fur
G oing into a magical, wonderful dimension
H er whole body glows and everything looks and tastes of chocolate
T he power of my peculiar pet is too magical to mention.

Isabella Gudice (9)
St Mary's RC Primary School, Swinton

Eleratpin

E leratpin is my stretchy pet
L oves eating cardboard, but very clever
E xtraordinary and different when she runs
R at and the legs of an elephant
A fter I have my tea, Eleratpin stomps and gets ready to play
T en years old, very gentle but messy
P ink is her skin colour, purple for its nails
I nsects are her friends
N or her or me like being inside.

Fabiana Race (9)
St Mary's RC Primary School, Swinton

The Flying Pig

F lying Pig, who is very big
L ives on a gigantic farm with other animals
Y es, he is big, with small thin feet
I t sees an angry bull charging at him
"**N** o!" shouted another animal. "Run!"
G alloping, the pig ran

P ig is very scared and hid
I nside the barn the pig is
G ot away in the end, safe and sound now.

Finn Mailey (9)
St Mary's RC Primary School, Swinton

The Girabull

Girabull is a very hungry and angry animal
It likes to wreck houses and it will sneak up on its prey
If you dare look at the darkness in its eyes
Then get prepared to die
Then you'll fly

He lives in the wild with the darkness of a cabinet
If any other animals' brains think they can get in the Girabull's habitat
they will be dead, so he can be fed.

Kalan Williams (9)
St Mary's RC Primary School, Swinton

The Snerbal

A snerbal is a very gentle pet
Whatever happens, don't take it to the vet
Its venomous bite could kill you in one crunch
If you are friends with it, it won't bite
Don't let it see another snerbal because it will fight
It is very clever and has sharp claws
But strangely, it roars
It is a very rare kind
and is really hard to find.

Harvey-Jay Mungins (10)
St Mary's RC Primary School, Swinton

Lightning, The Dog

Lightning is an extraordinary, cute and clever dog
Lightning can talk and lives with me
He can fly like a superhero
He eats dog food and he is very funny
Lightning is a marvellous and adorable dog
He is as fast as lightning
He is black and white and has sharp teeth
He can help you with everything.

Nicholas Bosak (9)
St Mary's RC Primary School, Swinton

The Eagrab

- **E** ating cute little kittens
- **A** ngry and evil, fast as a cheetah
- **G** rabs and pinches your clever cat
- **R** un, you better run or your arms say bye-bye
- **A** head of an eagle, the body of a clawed crab
- **B** e aware, it is harmful, you better scurry or he will eat your kitty.

Dawid Rachwal (10)
St Mary's RC Primary School, Swinton

Dird

D og's face, but really a bird
I n the wild living in a tree far, far away
R olling all over inside a tree just like a dog would do
D ird eats other animals and humans, also the dird flies.

Lucy Dyer (9)
St Mary's RC Primary School, Swinton

Sassy Rabbit

This creature is not so ordinary
Apart from spring when people say
That rabbit is absolutely extraordinary
What if I told you that was a lie
As the farmer next door wants it as rabbit pie
I know he's rather quite cheeky
I know that if people bought him
He would be seriously freaky
For the first few days, it would be quiet
The next would be an absolute riot
So the next time you want to get one at the store
Remember this tale, the rabbits are quite a bore
So if you do buy a rabbit, never have a sassy habit.

Amelia Williams (10)
St Michael With St Thomas Primary School, Widnes

My Household Pet, Roodie

Roodie is my household pet, who loves to eat my socks
They may be very tasty to him, but make his poops come out like rocks
Roodie is so curly, his hair is like a 'fro
He's crazy, smelly and naughty, but he's still my little bro
Roodie makes us laugh and smile, I take him for his walks
He barks, he sniffs and pees on walls, but I do enjoy his talks
My dog, Roodie, looks like a sheep, his hair is soft and fluffy
I can tell you one place to find him and that's at the front line of the buffet.

Ellis Welding (10)
St Michael With St Thomas Primary School, Widnes

All About Twinkles!

T winkles is a very small little hamster
W ild, she's always running on her wheel like mad
I ncredible, she's always rolling round in her food
N ever does she bite
K ind, Twinkles will always tickle you and maybe likes you
L azy, you can say that again, she's rushing but she's always sleeping
E ven though she's always eating and running
S mall, Twinkles is very small and she is a dwarf hamster.

Summer Cowen (10)
St Michael With St Thomas Primary School, Widnes

The Laser-Eyed Lizard!

Most lizards hunt with tongues and being sly
But my laser-eyed lizard hunts with beams from his eye
When hunger is his desire
His eyes begin to burn like fire
The pupils glow and a beam starts to grow
Like a mean, green shot
The poor cricket's legs become hot
Its body starts to burn
And into ash, it will soon turn
Ready to be eaten by the waiting reptile
My laser-eyed lizard called Kyle.

Hayden Vallender (10)
St Michael With St Thomas Primary School, Widnes

Funky Fish Friday

F unny goldfish who loves to party
U nusual goldfish that sings and dances
N ice fish who loves to drink seawater
K ind, caring fish
Y ellow and orange funny fish

F unky fish likes a good dance
I nk he drinks from the octopus' tentacles
S hy but funny crazy fish
H appy as can ever be.

Evie Halkett (10)
St Michael With St Thomas Primary School, Widnes

Spencer The Spiky, Scary Sloth

- **S** cary sloth on the tree
- **P** rowling cautiously
- **E** xtremely unordinary as you can see
- **N** imble eyes looking for his next victim
- **C** amouflaged through the trees, you can't even see him
- **E** xtremely hard to find in nature
- **R** umbling through the leaves.

India Mullarkey (10)
St Michael With St Thomas Primary School, Widnes

Our Baz

B ottle Top Barry loves to play with bottle lids
A mazingly, he is like Messi, dribbling with a football
R ound and round he goes, but nobody knows
R eally what's going down in the kitchen
Y our guess is as good as mine. He's my crazy cat!

Max Jones (10)
St Michael With St Thomas Primary School, Widnes

The Long Dog

There are dogs called sausage dogs
And they are pretty weird
They have long bodies and flat on the ground
They look like a sausage
And that is where the name comes from
Some people say they are normal, but I disagree.

Sean Mcloughlin (11)
St Michael With St Thomas Primary School, Widnes

Peculiar Pets

W eirdo is my pet's name
E veryone thinks it's weird
I an, my neighbour, does
R ebecca's the same
D on't get me started with Dan
O nly I think it's fine.

Phoebe Price (11)
St Michael With St Thomas Primary School, Widnes

The Cat That Was Scared To Climb

Once upon a time, not long ago
There was a ginger cat called Pogo
He was afraid to jump
He was afraid to climb
Having nine lives was a waste of time
His brothers and sisters aren't afraid.

Elise Highfield (10)
St Michael With St Thomas Primary School, Widnes

The Feathered Frog

Jumping was so hard for Flock
It always made her cry
She went to the highest rock
She wanted to jump so high
Flock soon learnt she couldn't jump
But her feathers made her fly.

Holly Hart (10)
St Michael With St Thomas Primary School, Widnes

Young Writers Information

We hope you have enjoyed reading this book – and that you will continue to in the coming years.

If you're a young writer who enjoys reading and creative writing, or the parent of an enthusiastic poet or story writer, do visit our website **www.youngwriters.co.uk**. Here you will find free competitions, workshops and games, as well as recommended reads, a poetry glossary and our blog. There's lots to keep budding writers motivated to write!

If you would like to order further copies of this book, or any of our other titles, then please give us a call or order via your online account.

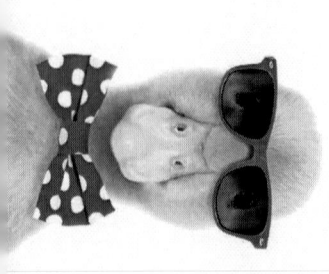

Young Writers
Remus House
Coltsfoot Drive
Peterborough
PE2 9BF
(01733) 890066
info@youngwriters.co.uk

Join in the conversation!
Tips, news, giveaways and much more!

YoungWritersUK   **@YoungWritersCW**